Cosenza Italy Travel Tips

Discover the most up-to-date and amazing places to sleep, eat, and shop in the Calabria region (Cosenza), along with essential information about the city

Hudson Miles

Table Of Contents

Visa

If you are not a citizen of a European Union (EU) or Schengen Area nation, you will usually need a visa to enter Italy. The reason and duration of your stay may necessitate a different visa.

Requirements may vary based on the type of visa (tourist, work, study, etc.). Generally, you'll need a completed application form, passport, passport-sized photos, travel itinerary, proof of accommodation, financial means, and, depending on the visa type, additional documents

Click on the link or scan the QR code.
https://vistoperitalia.esteri.it/home/en

You can also download the visa application form, fill it out, print it, and bring it to the Visa Application Centre for submission.
Refer to the details of the Tourist Office in this guide for additional personal information.

Cosenza

Cosenza, one of Calabria's major cities, has first-rate tourism facilities, but the nearby cities are just as breathtaking.

One of the oldest settlements in Calabria, Cosenza (also called the city of the Bruzios) is situated above seven hills that encircle the Crater Valley.

The city is slowly sloping downward. Situated on the Pancrácio Hill's slopes, it is situated in a scenic area at the meeting point of the Busento River, which separates the city's modern and ancient halves.

It was referred to as the Athens of Italy because of its rich cultural history.

Must See Cosenza

The cosentine area is diverse, with 155 towns that make up the first province of Calabria and a preponderance of hills and mountains mixed in with low areas and long sections of coastline.

With a 2,500-year history, the city of Bruzi is a must-visit location to relive the history of Alaric and the life of Frederick II of Swabia. It is located less than an hour's drive from the Ionian and Tyrrhenian Seas as well as the mountains of Sila and Pollino.

It is imperative to remain close to the town of Cosenza when taking a journey in these regions, since it undoubtedly offers a variety of interesting activities.

Going To Rossano Calabro

We began the tour in the Cosenza surrounds, making our first visit to Rossano Calabro. Situated on the Sibari Plain, between Sila and the stunning Ionian Sea shoreline, it overlooks the ocean.

Apart from the various structures dispersed over the city, the old town of Rossano houses a multitude of historic artworks left behind by the Greek colonists. The famous "Codex Purpureus Rossanensis," one of the oldest and most valuable Byzantine gospels, dating from the fifth century, with gold and silver uncials on a purple parchment, and the Cathedral of the Maria Santissima Aqueropita (Rossano's Cathedral) in the old town are both worth seeing.

The latter contains writings in Greek and fifteen miniatures that represent the gospel, making it a true masterpiece.
One of the best surviving Byzantine churches in Italy, St. Mark's Oratory was originally dedicated to St. Anastasia and is arguably Rossano's oldest structure, second only to the Cathedral. Next is the late Gothic-style Church of San Bernardino, which was the city's first Catholic church and contains Oliverio de Somma's grave.

The Church of Panagia, a tenth-century Byzantine church named for "Mary Most Holy," is one example; the Church of St. Francis of Paola, built in the sixteenth century, has a stunning cloister and a Renaissance gateway.

To Travel To Castellano Calabrio
We discovered another place to visit a few kilometres away, in the town of Corigliano Calabro. This city in the Cosenza province is said to have its roots in the 977 Arab invasion.
 This city, which has a historic section called the Saints area, is situated in the foothills of Sila Grega. It has a barred structure with charmingly small streets constructed in layers of a hill. Citrus, clear crops, and agricultural areas' fertility have all contributed to the

city's robust growth. Roberto il Guiscardo built the city's ancient castle in 1073 as a military stronghold.

Roberto Sanseverino, the Count of Corigliano, converted it into an aristocratic home in the middle of the fourteenth century. The archbishop of Rossano purchased the castle in 1971, and the city of Corigliano purchased it from them in 1979.
It's one of those structures whose historical significance has added to the town's charm.

Situated on the Gulf of Corigliano, which is the broader portion of the Gulf of Taranto, Corigliano is also home to the sole commercial fishing boat port of the upper Jonio Cosentino.

Going To Sybaris
We stayed close by to take in the views of the renowned Ancient Greek settlement of Sybaris, which is located between the rivers Crati (Crathis) and Coscile (Sybaris), on the Ionian Sea and overlooking the Gulf of Taranto.

A tiny town that today only makes up a small portion of its great and atavistic past, when it was dominated by the establishment of a thriving empire and the significant colony of Poseidonia, which the Romans later dubbed Paestum.

Today, tourism accounts for the majority of its economy. Akhaians from the Peloponnese founded Sybaris in the late eighth century between two rivers.

Unfortunately, Sybaris suffered from the same decline as all the other great empires in history due to the actions of the city of Crotone. The Sybaris National archaeological Museum currently houses the ancient city's archaeological remnants.

The greatest plain in Calabria, the plain of Sybaris, was revealed by the partnership Opera Sila, which led to the recovery of land and the subsequent rise of the city. It had a growth in seashore and cultural tourism in the 1980s and 1990s.

With its magnificent lagoon, engineering feat, and illustration of requalification of the land in conjunction with nature, Sybaris is a well-known tourist attraction for the Nautical Centre, "Sibari Lakes."

Going To Altomonte

Altomonte, a village in the province of Cosenza that is a member of the group "The most beautiful villages in Italy," is another close location that you should not miss. Situated around 455 metres above sea level, it is a promontory.

Its area is extremely fruitful, consisting of a hill with breathtaking views and pristine air, and a plain surrounded by the rivers Grondi, Fiumicello, and Esaro. Over the course of its history, the community has witnessed the migration of various people groups and civilizations. Its residents are thought to have relocated to the present site sometime between 800 and 1000 AD.

The Normans and Suevi ruled the region for a while, but it was during Anjou's administration that the settlement rose to prominence as a hub of remarkable importance for art, culture, and religion. Numerous witnesses from different churches and structures that still preserve the village's artistic and cultural legacy are there.

There are a number of places to visit, such the Church of Our Lady of Consolation, a rare example of Gothic art-angina with a huge window and a lovely doorway, or the picturesque mediaeval lanes. The open-air Theatre is currently the site of many festivals and events.

Take a stroll!

Following a short stroll through the heart of Cosenza, we will be able to sample the light and refreshing water from the thirteen-channel Fountain from the Zumpo aqueduct in Sila.

From there, we will continue along the Corso Telesio, which is home to the House of Cultures and the Cathedral of 1100.
 Meanwhile, in one of the seven hills (Pancrazio), there is the imposing Suevo Castle, an ancient fortress that once served as a shelter for Frederick II of Swabia, the emperor-tycoon known as the "Stupor Mundi," who was enamoured with the city of Cosenza.

Take a look at Suevo Castle

Built by Ruggero II in 1130, it was rendered completely useless by the earthquake that struck in 1184, but it was rebuilt by the Saracens on the ruins of the ancient citadel bruzia. The fortress rose to the peak of Mount Pancrazio. In 1239, Frederick II of Swabia, popularly known as Stupor Mundi, sent labourers to restore it by erecting an octagonal tower.

Completely decked out for the festivities, it served as a royal palace for the newlyweds Luigi III d'Anjou and Margherita di Savoia in 1443. The Swabia Castle's architecture was greatly influenced from that point on. It features an octagonal, angular tower rest and a rectangular plan with a central plaza, which is a distinctive style of Swabia construction.

See the Churches of the Cosenza
The cathedral of Cosenza, the Cloister of St. Francis of Assisi, and the church of St. Domenico, with its exquisite interior (1500), are among the numerous churches that illustrate the progression of history.

Constructed in 1140, the Cathedral of Cosenza is situated in the old town and underwent reconstruction following the devastating earthquake of 1184.
The grave of Queen Isabel of Aragon is located within. The exterior is Gothic in style, with three naves and a Latin cross inside. The naves are separated by enormous rectangular Romanesque-style pillars made of pink Mendicino stone, and on top of them are Byzantine-style geometric or natural friezes. There are two baroque-style

chapels in the nave on the left, which have larger floors than the other naves.

The sixteenth-century disease that nearly killed Cosenza's residents was averted by the Madonna Del Pilerio, the city's matron, whose Byzantine icon still stands in the first chapel. Isabella of Aragon's tomb is located in the left arm of the transept; it may have been constructed in the year 1200 by French labourers.

Another sarcophagus, known as the Coco, is located in the right nave and is likely the tomb of Enrico VII, Frederick II's rebellious son.

The Assassination Church of St. Francis

One of the town's oldest religious structures is the church dedicated to St. Francis of Assisi, which was constructed near to the monastery. Situated atop Mount Pancrazio, the convent is accessible from the higher section of the ancient town.

A Benedictine monastery's ruins served as the foundation for it. After being completely destroyed by the earthquake in 1184, Frederick II repaired it and gave it to Peter Cathin, a friend and follower of St. Francis, to serve as the Friars Minor's house.

After a few years, the conventual Benedictines made their way back, followed by the smaller observers who constructed the Chapel of the Immaculate. The cloister, which is next to the church, was most likely built in 1436 by the observers, who inhabited the area. Encased in gilded oak, the greatest altar is located in the splendid interior. In the first half of 1900, the exquisitely carved wooden pulpit was created.

The San Domenico Church

The genuine contour line separating Cosenza's most contemporary and oldest neighbourhoods may be seen on Piazza Tommaso Campanella. Constructed on the site of a previous cult building dedicated to St. Matthew and consecrated in 1468, the religious building, which is part of a monastery complex built by Sanseverino's orders in the mid-fifteenth century, stands out over the square with its imposing baroque copper-clad cupola after World War II.

It flanked the Dominican monastery inside the palace that Sanseverino donated to the Dominicans. The rosette and the gate frame are two examples of the original Gothic-style elements that have been preserved on the exterior despite the renovations made to the original construction throughout the eighteenth century.

Dominican Convent

The historic Dominican monastery lies to the left of the cathedral. It features a stunning cloister with Catalan-Durazzo-style arches, pillars, and portals. In the middle is a well decorated with the coats of arms of Ferrari di Epaminonda and the Ruffo family. Constructed in 1449 according to the will of Antonio Sanseverino, the prince of Bisignano, who died in 1525, it housed the General Studio of the two Calabrian provinces, Citra and Ultra, where Tommaso Campanella was also located. After being suppressed in 1809, it served as the Military District seat before being purchased by the Cosenza Municipal Administration and used as a venue for cultural events.

Take a Look at The National Library

Visit the National Library, the Arnone Truglio Palace on Mount Truglio, which was once the court and prison and has been restored to its former splendour. Here, one can view the original icon of Madonna del Pilerio, matron of Cosenza, and the Estauroteca, a priceless reliquary that Frederick II gave to the city in honour of the Cathedral's restoration in 1222.

Other notable works in the collection are those by several southern painters, including Peter Negroni, Mattia Preti, and Luca Giordano.

Go to Cosenza's Stauroteca

The Stauroteca of Cosenza is an extremely valuable gold work that is embellished with enamels and priceless stones. The Stauroteca of Cosenza, which derives its name from the Greek words Stauròs, which means cross, and Heke, which means collection, is regarded as one of the most priceless pieces of art on display in Calabria.

 It is a cross reliquary that holds a piece of the real cross of Christ and is among the most exquisite and valuable in the entire world. On January 30, 1222, this significant relic was given to Cosenza by Emperor Frederick II of Swabia as a gift during the Cathedral's consecration ceremony following the disastrous earthquake that occurred in 1184.

A bit of History (Cosenza)

Cosenza is a historic city that is softly sprawled over the seven hills that surround it. It is said that with the arrival of Emperor Frederick II in Cosenza in 1222, the city and the neighbouring territories were bestowed with symbols and insignia that symbolised them. The seven hills that round the location where the "village" has grown for thousands of years were selected by the people of Cosenza to serve as their city's symbol.

He always enjoyed drawing parallels between Rome and the most well-known Seven Hills, so it's safe to say that this call had an impact on his decision. The old city of Cosenza was situated on the seven hills, which are organised as follows: Crati, Pancrazio, Torrevetere, Guarassano, Triglio, Venneri, Gramazio, and Mussano. These hills were formed prior to the development of the northern plains.

Cosenza, a stunning city in Calabria, has its roots in the time when almost bretti chose to establish their capital at the base of the Silano plateau. It is situated in an area once inhabited by old noble people and frequently visited by the Romans. It is believed that Alaric, the Visigoth monarch, died there in 411 AD from malaria, and scholars from all over the world are still looking for him. From that point on, a sequence of historically significant and dramatic events took place as a result of the earthquakes, which frequently decimated the numerous dominions that followed: the Lombards in 579 AD, the Saracens in 864 AD, and the Byzantines in AD 958.

The Normans arrived in 1058 and left their mark on the castle. When the Suevi returned, the emperor Frederick II, who stayed there until 1271, reconstructed the Norman castle on the ruins and constructed the magnificent Cosenza Cathedral in 1150. The Aragons started the lengthy Spanish dominance in 1284, and the Bourbons terminated it in 1735.

A Further Explanation Of Cosenza

The Piedmonts, in particular, moved industrial and artisanal areas to work steel, silk, and tannin; these thriving businesses in the northern regions left an unaltered balance of landowners.

The Piedmonts did not behave any differently from other newcomers. In other words, in accordance with the "best" political tradition, which calls for people to think about the good and to exchange favours, they eliminated those who could (artisans) and who were no longer able (the Bourbons) to leave to the powerful (the barons).

Unfortunately, we are all too familiar with the support that culture evolved under such circumstances for the poor and obedient Calabrian people.

After that, Cosenza spread throughout Mount Pancrazio and discovered that, during the 20-year fascist period (1923–1945), safety regulations that had previously required it to establish itself on the hill could no longer impede its natural growth.

It was the first city to fly the tricolour flag in 1820, and it endured the horrors of the inquisition in addition to giving birth to notable individuals like Tommaso Campanella. Numerous uprisings and violent incidents, including the dismissal of the Bandeira brothers in the Rovito Valley, took place there.

Among Cosenza's many historical snippets, there are remnants that evoke the colossal pieces that endure to this day. Of all the summits, the Norman Suevo Castle, which dates from 1110 to 1210, is located atop Mount Pancrazio and nearly seems to be a witness to history's passage through the ages.

How do I get there?
- How do I get there? VIA PLANE

The closest airport to Cosenza is Lamezia Terme, which is 77 km away and reachable by bus, train, and taxi. The Crotone Airport has direct bus and/or train connections to Cosenza.

- How do I get there? VIA TRAIN

The Intercity or Espresso of Cosenza departs straight from the Rome or Naples station; the Intercity or Espresso of Rome-Napoli is an additional option. Reggio Calabria, station Paola (36 km from Cosenza), then take the connection to Cosenza; to reach the old town from the train station, take an urban bus service.

From Reggio Calabria, you can go directly, via Espresso or Intercity, to Cosenza, or by train from Reggio Calabria – Napoli, station Paola, which connects to Cosenza.

- The way there? VIA VEHICLE

Route A3: leave, then go north and south through Cosenza (522 km south of Rome).

Let's Conclude

Situated on the slopes of Mount Pancrazio, Cosenza lies in the Valley of the Crati, surrounded by a natural frame of hills at the meeting point of the Busento river, which separates the city's modern and ancient halves. With the city's distinctive Mediterranean climate and its many artistic, historical, and cultural wonders, there is never a bad time to visit.

This valley, which encircles Sila to the east, the sea mountain to the west, the Massif of Pollino to the north, and the Savuto hills to the south, is the best route to access the province's many regions.

With its 2,500-year history, the city of Bruzia is a must-see destination to relive the history of Alaric, the life of Frederick II of Swabia (Stupor Mundi), the Cathedral, the Suevo Castle, and all of its downtown can be reached in less than an hour by car, passing by the Ionian and Tyrrhenian Seas as well as the mountains of Sila and Pollino.

This city is appealing not just because of its history, culture, and artwork, but also because of its cuisine, customs, warmth, and breathtaking surroundings, which will stay with you forever.

In any case, Cosenza—dubbed the "Milan of the south" today—has an advantage over the other capital cities of Calabria since it is the most livable despite a host of issues.

Athletics
The Cosenza Calcio football team, in Serie B, is based in Cosenza.

Celebrations And Festivities
Marche, Fiera di S. Giuseppe
July: Festival delle Invasioni
October marks the Chocolate Festival, or Festa del Cioccolato.
Wine Festival (Sagra dell'uva e del vino) in Donnici, October

Tourist Office

- Mappa Tattile Piazza Bilotti
- Location: Corso G. Mazzini

- World In The City Di Pasqua Luca & C. S.A.S.
- Location: Viale della Repubblica, 30
- Phone: +39 0984 062661

- Associazione N.9
- Location: Via Pasquale Galluppi, 15
- Phone: +39 338 920 5394

- GuideInCalabria di Alessandra Scanga - Guida Turistica Abilitata
- Location: Via Vittorio Veneto, 58
- Phone: +39 329 445 2028

Attractions

Below are more Attractions in the city, both popular and lesser-known ones. Visit any of them, depending on your preference.

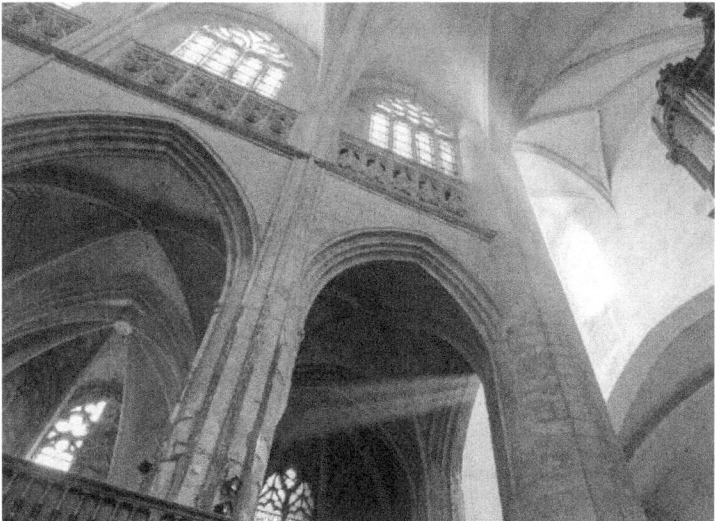

- • - Fontana di Cosenza:
Landmark fountain located in Piazza Europa, 14, offering a refreshing sight in the heart of the city.

- • - MAB Cosenza - Museo all'Aperto Bilotti:
Outdoor museum along Corso G. Mazzini showcasing contemporary art installations.

- - Museo Multimediale Città di Cosenza:
Multimedia museum situated in P.za Carlo Bilotti, offering insights into the city's history and culture.

- - Museum of Brettii and Enotri:
Cultural attraction at Vico Sant'Agostino, 3, showcasing artefacts from ancient Brettii and Enotri civilizations.

- - Parco delle Civiltà Maestre:
Tranquil park located at Via Giovanni Macchione, 1, celebrating various ancient civilizations.

- - Centro storico di Cosenza:
Historic center along Corso Telesio, 45, featuring charming streets and buildings dating back centuries.

- - Murale Le tre donne:
Artistic mural depicting three women, located at Via Luigi Vercillo, 1, adding vibrancy to the city's streets.

- - Il cammino di San Francesco:
Spiritual trail at Via Porta Piana, 97, following in the footsteps of Saint Francis of Assisi.

- - Bronzi di Riace, di Sasha Sosno:
 Sculptural installation on Corso G. Mazzini, 262/272, showcasing the famous Riace Bronzes.

- - Murale a Bernardino Telesio:

Artistic mural located at Viale Giacomo Mancini, 829, honoring Bernardino Telesio, a philosopher from Cosenza.

- - Museo Del Fumetto:
Comic book museum at Via Liceo, 1, celebrating the art and history of comics.

- - Murale "I due ragazzi e il Pandino":
Artistic mural at Via Antonio Ferrari Di Epaminonda, 7, depicting two youths and the Pandino fountain.

- - Norman Castle:
Historic castle on Colle Pancrazio, offering panoramic views of the city (temporarily closed).

- - Presepe nell'albero:
Nativity scene located at Viale della Repubblica, 221, adding festive cheer during the holiday season.

- - Murale Dea Atena:
Artistic mural at Via Tommaso Aceti, 11, depicting the goddess Athena, symbolizing wisdom and strength.

- - Calabria Towers Tour:
Touristic experience in Diodato, Province of Cosenza, Italy, showcasing the region's ancient watchtowers.

- - Murale Le due Fioraie:
Artistic mural at Via Luigi Vercillo, 1, depicting two flower vendors, adding color to the city streets.

- - Murale Thelma and Louise:

Artistic mural at Via Roberto Mirabelli, 3, paying homage to the iconic characters from the movie.

- - Palazzo della Provincia:

Provincial palace located at Piazza XV Marzo, 5, showcasing impressive architecture and historical significance.

- - Piazza Carlo Bilotti ex Piazza Luigi Fera:

Formerly known as Piazza Luigi Fera, this square now bears the name Piazza Carlo Bilotti, retaining its charm and character.

Leisure Activities

Below are activities to get involved in, suggestions on day trips and excursions, Embark on any of these activities to enhance your travel experience.

- Cosenza Cathedral:
Immerse yourself in the rich history and stunning architecture of Cosenza's iconic cathedral located in Piazza Duomo.

- - Galleria Nazionale di Cosenza:
Explore a treasure trove of art at this national gallery showcasing works from various periods and styles.

- - Museo all'aperto Bilotti (Mab):

Take a leisurely stroll through the open-air museum along Corso Giuseppe Mazzini, featuring captivating contemporary art installations.

- - Centro Storico:

Wander through the charming historic center of Cosenza along Corso Bernardino Telesio, where centuries of history come alive amidst picturesque streets and buildings.

- - Castello Normanno-Svevo:

Step back in time as you visit this imposing Norman-Swabian castle, offering panoramic views of the city and a glimpse into its medieval past.

- - Corso Mazzini:

Experience the bustling heart of Cosenza along this vibrant street, lined with shops, cafes, and historic landmarks.

- - Stadio San Vito - Gigi Marulla:

Catch a thrilling football match or soak up the lively atmosphere at this stadium, home to Cosenza Calcio.

- - Lanificio Leo:

Discover the fascinating history of textile production at this unique museum located in Soveria Mannelli, just a short distance from Cosenza.

- - Castello Ducale:

Journey to the nearby town of Corigliano Calabro to explore this majestic Ducal castle, offering a glimpse into the region's feudal past.

- - Isola Di Cirella:

Escape to the picturesque Isola Di Cirella, where crystal-clear waters, pristine beaches, and rugged cliffs await exploration.

- - MAM - Museo delle Arti e dei Mestieri:

Delve into the traditional arts and crafts of Cosenza at this museum, housed in a historic building along Corso Bernardino Telesio.

- - Villa Rendano:

Take a moment to admire the elegant architecture and lush gardens of Villa Rendano, a tranquil oasis in the heart of Cosenza.

- - Teatro di tradizione Alfonso Rendano:

Immerse yourself in the vibrant cultural scene of Cosenza at this historic theater, hosting a variety of performances throughout the year.

When travelling, it's advisable to book your tours in advance if interested. Consider using Viator (https://www.viator.com/) for great deals. Scan the QR code to book online.

General information

Emergency Numbers: Dial 112 for all-hazards help.
- 113 (accidents, thefts, and police problems).
- Fire Department: 115 (for fire emergencies and weather-related difficulties).
- Urgent Medical Attention: 118 (for medical crises or mountain or cave rescue).
- Roadside Assistance (ACI): 803.116.

To call Italy, dial the international code +39 followed by the number.
- To make an international call from Italy, dial 00 followed by the international code and number.

Purchasing an Italian SIM card for cost-effective communication is recommended.

Tips

- Exercise care at night, at train stations, airports, and in congested places.
- Be on the lookout for pickpockets, especially if they seem to be well-dressed.
- Be cautious while drinking extensively to prevent being a victim of crime.

Packing Suggestions

Best Luggage & Bags: - A hard-sided suitcase for long-term use.
   - For carry-on, a sturdy backpack or a lightweight shoulder bag.
   - A fashionable crossbody bag for tiny necessities.
   - A tote bag made of canvas or mesh for adaptability.

What to Bring in Your Carry-On Bag
- A valid passport and, if necessary, a visa.
- Cash and credit cards are accepted.
- An extra pair of pants for unexpected layovers.

Headphones or noise-cancelling earphones are recommended for in-flight use.
- A sleep mask to help you sleep throughout the journey.
- A shawl, pashmina, or travel blanket to keep you warm.
- For amusement, use an iPad or a lightweight laptop.

Basic One-Week Packing List
- A variety of tank tops, tees, blouses, and long-sleeve tops.
- Jeans, black or neutral trousers and a lightweight jacket are all appropriate.
- Pants, yoga pants and sweatshirts.
- Sneakers and more formal shoes, sunglasses and a water bottle.

Seasonal Additions
-**Spring**: raincoat, scarves and a travel umbrella.
   Summer attire includes sundresses, shorts, swimsuits, flip-flops and sunscreen.
- In the **autumn**, bring a warm hat, scarf, additional layers, a travel umbrella and boots.
- In the **winter**, bring a winter coat, additional layers, gloves, and toiletries.

Packing toiletries for pain alleviation, constipation, diarrhoea, and motion sickness.

What NOT to Bring
Valuables and expensive jewellery to prevent pickpocketing.
  - Full-sized toiletries; choose travel-sized or half-used goods instead.
  - Hairdryer and heat styling gadgets; most hotels provide them.

Last but not least, pack smartly with appropriate footwear and gear for the season. - Have a wonderful time in Italy.

Planning
Best Time to Visit: From April to June, the weather is great, avoiding the sweltering heat of summer. Late spring has a bright sky and less people.

Considerations for Summer: July and August are peak months, with crowded beaches and increased pricing. Prepare for hot weather by planning and booking ahead of time.

Autumn Delights: From September to November, the weather is mild and the landscape is beautiful. Take advantage of cuisine festivals, wine harvests, and cultural activities.

Winter Attractions: Snow activities are popular in the Alps from December to March. Winter also offers Christmas markets, New Year's Eve events, and reduced off-season travel expenses.

Practical Information

Holiday Season: Italians often travel on vacation in August, resulting in crowded beaches, business closures, and increased pricing. Plan ahead of time, particularly near Ferragosto on August 15.

While Italy is a car-centric country, public transit is both economical and dependable. Renting a vehicle allows independence, yet trains and buses successfully link major centres.

Car Rental scarcity: Due to the pandemic, there is a rental car scarcity. Book early, particularly during high holiday seasons.

Card payments are typically accepted, however bringing cash is recommended for occasional outliers. The majority of major credit card networks are accepted.

Regional Pride: Celebrate regional pride (campanilismo) by learning about how inhabitants take pride in their own locations, which provide unique experiences and flavours.

Sarcasm in Humour: Sarcasm and self-deprecation are often used in Italian humour. Expect clever conversation, particularly in locations such as Veneto or Tuscany.

Hand Gestures: Italians use expressive hand gestures to communicate. Learn the meanings of the gestures to prevent misunderstandings, since each gesture carries different information.

Restaurant Etiquette: Don't be intimidated by lengthy

menus. You are not required to order from each area. You may mix and combine dishes as you want.

Tipping Culture: Tipping is not required, although it is appreciated for outstanding service. Some restaurants may levy "coperto" fees.

Timing of Eating and Drinking: Stick to local conventions such as drinking a coffee in the morning, an Aperol Spritz before dinner, and limoncello after meals. Lunch is served at 1pm, while supper is served around 8pm.

Drinking in Public: Drinking alcohol in public is legal and widespread in many places. Outdoor drinking, particularly in public squares, is an important aspect of local social life.

Cheek Kissing Etiquette: In casual contexts, Italians often greet with cheek kisses. Pay attention to social clues, and if you're uneasy, a simple handshake will be enough.

Political Awareness: Political polarisation is increasing in Italy. Be cognizant of opposing viewpoints, particularly in conversations like migration, energy, housing, and workers' rights. Political debates may be heated, so read the room appropriately.

Budget Travel in Italy
Fly into minor airports provided by low-cost airlines; consider alternate transit choices, such as high-speed trains linking big cities.

Travel during the shoulder seasons (May, June,

September, and October) to balance weather, prices, and avoid peak crowds.

Taking Public transit vs Renting a Car: Taking public transit is a more cost-effective option to explore cities.
  - Save money by purchasing high-speed rail tickets in advance, and think about multi-day travel passes.

Affordable Dining: For low-cost lunches, look for fixed-price lunch menus at trattorias.
  - To avoid extra service costs, order your espresso at the bar.

Water and Beverages: Drink tap water to save money and limit your use of plastic.
  - When sitting at cafés, be in mind that service costs may apply.

Art & Cultural Exploration: Schedule art excursions during off-seasons to save money on museum admission.
  - Visit churches to see free exhibits of famous artworks.

- Look for "free" beaches (spiaggia libera) to avoid paying rental fees at private beaches.
  - Ask around for information on free beach places that are accessible.

Pilgrimages on a Budget: Consider hiking or bicycling along traditional pilgrimage routes such as the Via Francigena.
  - For less expensive lodging, stay in monasteries or pilgrim hostels.

Average Daily Costs: - Budget at least €130 a day to cover key attractions, lunches, and transportation.

Alternative Lodging Options: - Look into low-cost options such as hostels or agriturismi (farm stays).
   - For multi-day rail travel, use the **Trenitalia Pass**.

Off-Peak Art Exploration: During the off-season, prominent art institutions offer cheap admission.

Transportation Savings Tip
Fly with low-cost carriers such as **Ryanair, WizzAir, EasyJet, or Vueling**.
   - Consider overland entrance or intercity travel via high-speed trains.

Environmental and financial savings may be obtained by drinking tap water and avoiding the use of single-use plastics.

Exploring Italy on a budget entails making smart decisions about travel seasons, means of transportation, food alternatives, and cultural discovery to ensure a cheap but meaningful trip.

Transportation and Visa

Visas are not required for citizens of Schengen nations, the EU, or the EAA.

   - Around 60 non-EU countries, including the United Kingdom, the United States, Canada, Japan, Australia, and others, have visa-free travel for up to 90 days during any 180-day period.

- Other countries need a Schengen visa; application procedures differ.

Working Holiday Visa: Italy grants working holiday visas to young people aged 18 to 30 from Australia, Japan, New Zealand, South Korea, and Canada.

Local Transportation: - Trenitalia and Italo maintain an extensive rail network linking key cities in Italy.
- Buses serve regions that are not served by trains, while long-distance coaches are controlled by commercial firms such as **Flixbus**.
- Ferries are used to link islands and coastal regions.

Driving in Italy: - Renting a car, motorbike or Vespa provides freedom, particularly in rural regions.
- Roads are divided into several groups with varied speed restrictions.
- Potholes, traffic, and parking issues are all possible driving circumstances.

Domestic flights are possible, however they are often less convenient than trains or buses.
- Airlines such as ITA Airways, easyJet, and Ryanair fly into major cities.

Cycling: Cycling pathways, including electric bike alternatives, are available throughout Italy.
- Road cycling is popular in Northern Italy, particularly in the Alps and Dolomites.

Accessibility: While Italy is developing accessibility, there are still obstacles for impaired travellers.
- Some trains and buses provide help to disabled passengers.

- Village for All and Fondazione Cesare Serono are two online organisations that give information about accessible amenities and beaches.

Travel Insurance
When travelling to Italy, I use and suggest **World Nomads.**

Do you know?
The top Two Restaurants in Italy are Chefs Massimo Bottura (Osteria Francescana) and Niko Romito (Reale)

Tourists throws more than €1,000,000 into the Trevi Fountain each year

Pizza was invented in Naples

Italy is the world's largest wine producer

It's bad Omen to place bread upside down on the table.

Common hand gestures in Italy

- Raised Index Finger: Used to get someone's attention or emphasize a point.

- Chin Flick: A quick flick of the chin with the fingers, often used to express indifference or dismissal.

- Hand Purse (Fingers Kissing): Fingers brought together in a kissing motion, indicating perfection, excellence, or approval.

- Thumb and Fingers Pinched Together: Signifying that something is expensive or costly.

- Clenched Fist with Raised Arm: A gesture of victory or success.

- Cheek Pinch: Gently pinching the cheek of a child or someone close as a sign of affection.

- Shrugging Shoulders: A universal gesture of expressing uncertainty or not knowing.

- Italian Hand Gesture (Fingers Together, Shaking Side to Side): Expressing uncertainty, disbelief, or disagreement.

- Hand on Heart: Placing the hand on the chest to emphasize sincerity or truthfulness.

Scan the QR code below and search for the Location you are going to in Italy and have a better view. Safe travels.

The map is the same on your phone. Consider taking screenshots as you walk around with no connection needed. Alternatively, you can contact the tourist office using the addresses and numbers provided in this guide.

Write down your activities in the box below

Day 1	Day 2	Day 3
Arrival (hotel) and Acquaintance	Adventure (leisure) and relaxation	Explore and Farewell

Write down your activities in the box below

Day 4	Day 5	Day 6
Arrival (hotel) and Acquaintance	Adventure (leisure) and relaxation	Explore and Farewell

In most cases, I use the Wanderlog website or app to plan my trip itinerary and expenses. You can try it if you're interested. Click the link below or scan the QR code to create a new account.

https://wanderlog.com

Transportation

Below are recommended Transportation related services in the city. It is advisable to make reservations online at **omio.com** or by scanning the QR code.

Transport Services

Below are recommended transportation-related services in the city. Contact them if necessary upon landing at the nearby airport. It is advisable to make reservations online at omio.com or by scanning the QR code above.

- • - Transport Italia Romania:
 Provides transportation services for passengers and cargo between cities in Italy and various destinations in Calabria, including Napoli, Roma, and Cosenza. . Phone: +39 380 346 4331.

- • - Noleggio con conducente Cosenza Taxi:
Offers taxi services with professional drivers in Castrolibero, Province of Cosenza, Italy. . Phone: +39 329 385 7243.

- Cosenza Taxi 01: Taxi service available in Cosenza. . Phone: +39 368 236 058.

- - TAXI/NCC Ditta Curcio:
  Taxi service operating in Quattromiglia, Province of Cosenza, Italy, providing transportation services with experienced drivers. . Phone: +39 348 336 8260.

- - Transfer Calabria:
  Offers transportation services 24/7 throughout Calabria. Located at Via Calabria, sn. Phone: +39 351 920 6500.

- - Cosenza Taxi NCC:
  Transportation service available at Cosenza Railway Station. Address: Stazione Ferroviaria di Cosenza. Phone: +39 347 653 9158.

- - Buses Preite srl:
  Local bus and coach company providing services from Viale Delle Medaglie D'Oro, 42. Phone: +39 0984 413001.

- - Autostazione:
  Transit station located at Viale Delle Medaglie D'Oro, 11, offering bus services.

Hotels

When traveling, it's advisable to book your hotel in advance.

Consider using Booking.com for great deals, available for select hotels worldwide. Scan the QR code to book online. Here are some recommended hotels to consider:

- • - Italiana Hotels Cosenza
- Location: Via Panebianco, 452
- Phone: +39 0984 175 8042

- Chic hotel with complimentary parking and Wi-Fi, Mediterranean restaurant, pool, and gym facilities.

- - Royal Hotel
- Location: Via Delle Medaglie D'Oro, Via XXIV Maggio, 1
- Phone: +39 0984 412165
- Relaxed lodging providing free breakfast and Wi-Fi, featuring a restaurant, bar, and lounge.

- - Hotel Excelsior
- Location: Piazza Giacomo Matteotti, 14
- Phone: +39 0984 74383
- Neoclassical building offering modest rooms and suites, restaurant, bar, and breakfast.

- - Home Club Suite Hotel
- Location: 26/N, Viale Giacomo Mancini
- Phone: +39 0984 178 2529
- Chic hotel with modern suites featuring kitchenettes, along with a contemporary restaurant and bar.

- - Palace Eight - Suites & Spa
- Location: Via Giuseppe Galliano, 4
- Phone: +39 366 107 6850
- Luxurious suites and spa facilities for a relaxing stay.

- - Epoca Home
- Location: Corso G. Mazzini, 264
- Phone: +39 351 869 2360
- Elegant accommodations in a central location.

Restaurants

Try any of the top recommended restaurants known for their pleasant services, mouthwatering menus, and reasonable prices. You can reach them through the provided contact details.

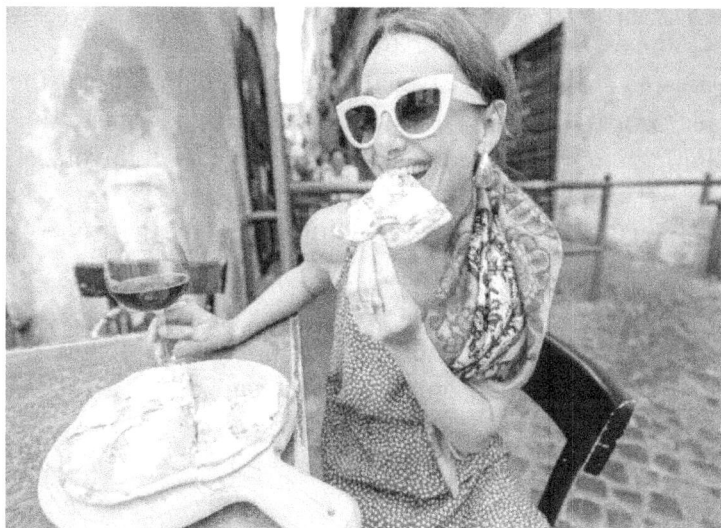

- - Al Girone Dei Golosi Ristorante Enoteca
- Location: Via Pasquale Rossi, 79
- Phone: +39 0984 394859
- - Italian eatery showcasing Calabrian specialties like swordfish and Calabrese pizza, prepared with local ingredients and flavors.

- - Calabria Bella
- Location: Piazza Duomo, 20
- Phone: +39 0984 793531
- - Italian restaurant offering traditional dishes such as pasta with 'nduja and Caciocavallo cheese, crafted with authentic Calabrian ingredients.

- - Le 3 Forchette
- Location: Via Isonzo, 15
- Phone: +39 0984 152 4963
- - Restaurant specialising in Calabrian cuisine, featuring dishes like Cipolle di Tropea and Pepperoncini-infused pasta, showcasing local flavors.

- - Tabernacolo Cosenza Bistro Pub
- Location: Corso G. Mazzini, 159/D
- Phone: +39 351 919 5581
- - Casual pub offering a variety of Italian dishes and drinks, perfect for enjoying local cuisine in a relaxed atmosphere.

Shopping

Below are recommendable shops in the city.
Explore shopping in any of these stores and bring back
some souvenirs.

- • - La City Shopping Center
  - Type: Shopping mall
  - Address: Via Panebianco, 436
  - - A bustling shopping center offering a variety of
stores and boutiques for all your shopping needs.

- • - I Due Fiumi • centro commerciale
  - Type: Shopping mall
  - Address: Piazza Giacomo Mancini, 33

- - Vibrant shopping destination featuring diverse shops and eateries in a central location.

- - Metropolis Shopping Mall
 - Type: Shopping mall
 - Address: Rende, Province of Cosenza, Italy
 - Phone: +39 0984 462707
 - - Expansive mall hosting popular brands and dining options, providing a diverse shopping experience.

- - Mille Scelte
 - Type: Shopping mall
 - Address: Via Popilia, 29
 - - Shopping complex offering a wide selection of products and services in a convenient location.

- - Armazem Outlet
 - Type: Clothing store
 - Address: Corso G. Mazzini, 198
 - Phone: +39 0984 795245
 - - Outlet store featuring discounted clothing items and accessories from various brands.

- - Store Cosenza Calcio
 - Type: Sportswear store
 - Address: Via Arabia
 - Phone: +39 0984 152 3527
 - - Sports apparel shop specialising in Cosenza Calcio merchandise and sportswear essentials.

- • - Vestium Fashion Outlet
- Type: Outlet mall
- Address: Quattromiglia, Province of Cosenza, Italy
- Phone: +39 0984 190 2933
- - Fashion outlet offering discounted designer clothing and accessories in a spacious setting.

- • - Timberland Store Cosenza
- Type: Clothing store
- Address: Piazza XI Settembre, Via Calabria, 10
- Phone: +39 0984 793331
- - Timberland outlet store providing quality outdoor clothing and footwear for adventure enthusiasts.

- • - Civetterie
- Type: Women's clothing store
- Address: Via Calabria, 30
- Phone: +39 0984 22512
- - Boutique offering trendy and stylish women's clothing and accessories for fashion-conscious shoppers.

- • - The Apartment
- Type: Women's clothing store
- Address: Corso G. Mazzini, 71
- Phone: +39 0984 24605
- - Chic boutique showcasing a curated collection of women's clothing and accessories for sophisticated tastes.

- • - Thun Shop
- Type: Novelty store

- Address: Via Monte Santo, 52
- Phone: +39 0984 274 0234
  - - Quaint store offering a variety of unique and charming gifts, home decor, and collectibles.

Phrases And Slang Terms

Basic Italian phrases and area slang terms to be familiar with before traveling.

- Buongiorno! - Good morning!
- Buonasera! - Good evening!
- Ciao! - Hello!
- Grazie! - Thank you!
- Prego! - You're welcome!
- Mi scusi! - Excuse me!
- Parla inglese? - Do you speak English?

- Posso avere il conto, per favore? - Can I have the bill, please?
- Dov'è il bagno? - Where is the bathroom?
- Quanto costa questo? - How much does this cost?
- Vorrei ordinare... - I would like to order...
- Mi può aiutare? - Can you help me?
- Mi sono perso/a. - I am lost.

- Sto cercando... - I am looking for...
- Vorrei una mappa della città. - I would like a map of the city.
- Dove posso trovare un bancomat? - Where can I find an ATM?
- Mi potrebbe consigliare un buon ristorante? - Could you recommend a good restaurant?

- Che ore sono? - What time is it?
- Posso pagare con carta di credito? - Can I pay with a credit card?
- Vorrei prenotare una camera. - I would like to book a room.

- Mi può chiamare un taxi, per favore? - Could you call me a taxi, please?
- Mi potrebbe dare indicazioni per...? - Could you give me directions to...?
- Che tempo fa oggi? - What is the weather like today?
- Mi potrebbe consigliare qualche attrazione da visitare?

- Could you recommend some attractions to visit?
- Mi scusi, non capisco. - I'm sorry, I don't understand.
- Mi potrebbe ripetere, per favore? - Could you repeat that, please?
- Dove si trova la stazione ferroviaria/autobus? - Where is the train/bus station?
- Quanto tempo ci vuole per arrivare a...? - How long does it take to get to...?
- Vorrei noleggiare una macchina. - I would like to rent a car.

- Ho bisogno di un medico. - I need a doctor.
- Mi piace molto questo posto. - I really like this place.
- Vorrei acquistare un biglietto per... - I would like to buy a ticket for...
- Mi piace molto la cucina italiana. - I really like Italian cuisine.

- Sto cercando un negozio di souvenir. - I am looking for a souvenir shop.
- È delizioso! - It's delicious!
- Questo è troppo caro. - This is too expensive.
- Potrebbe fare uno sconto? - Could you give me a discount?

- Vorrei fare una prenotazione. - I would like to make a reservation.
- Mi può consigliare un buon vino locale? - Can you recommend a good local wine?
- Dove posso trovare un internet café? - Where can I find an internet café?
- C'è un mercato qui vicino? - Is there a market nearby?
- Mi può consigliare un buon gelato? - Can you recommend a good gelato?

- Sto cercando un posto tranquillo per rilassarsi. - I am looking for a quiet place to relax.
- Ho bisogno di cambiare dei soldi. - I need to exchange some money.
- Vorrei fare un giro turistico della città. - I would like to take a sightseeing tour of the city.
- Quanto tempo rimane aperto? - How long is it open for?
- Vorrei noleggiare una bicicletta. - I would like to rent a bike.

- Mi potrebbe portare alla stazione, per favore? - Could you take me to the station, please?

- Dove posso trovare un posto per dormire? - Where can I find a place to sleep?
- È possibile pagare in contanti? - Is it possible to pay in cash?

- Posso usare il tuo telefono? - Can I use your phone?
- Sto cercando un museo. - I am looking for a museum.
- È incluso nel prezzo? - Is it included in the price?
- Potrebbe dirmi come tornare in albergo? - Could you tell me how to get back to the hotel?
- Mi potrebbe consigliare un buon libro? - Can you recommend a good book?

- C'è un supermercato qui vicino? - Is there a supermarket nearby?
- Vorrei noleggiare uno scooter. - I would like to rent a scooter.
- È aperto oggi? - Is it open today?
- Vorrei una bottiglia d'acqua. - I would like a bottle of water.
- Dove posso trovare un ufficio postale? - Where can I find a post office?

- Mi potrebbe consigliare un bel posto per fare una passeggiata? - Could you recommend a nice place for a walk?
- Potrebbe chiamare un taxi per domani mattina? - Could you call a taxi for tomorrow morning?
- Posso avere un menu in inglese, per favore? - Can I have a menu in English, please?

- Dove posso trovare una farmacia? - Where can I find a pharmacy?

- Vorrei visitare una chiesa. - I would like to visit a church.

- Posso fare una prenotazione per stasera? - Can I make a reservation for tonight?

- Posso avere una mappa della città? - Can I have a map of the city?

- È possibile noleggiare una guida turistica? - Is it possible to hire a tour guide?

- Sto cercando un ristorante con cucina tipica. - I am looking for a restaurant with local cuisine.

- Mi potrebbe consigliare un buon posto per fare shopping? - Could you recommend a good place for shopping?

- Posso pagare con carta di credito? - Can I pay by credit card?

- È incluso il servizio? - Is the service included?

- Dove posso trovare un distributore di benzina? - Where can I find a gas station?

- Vorrei una camera per stasera. - I would like a room for tonight.

- Mi può consigliare un buon posto per una cena romantica? - Can you recommend a good place for a romantic dinner?

- Posso avere un'informazione? - Can I have some information?

- Cosa mi consiglia di fare qui? - What do you recommend doing here?

- Mi può portare al centro della città? - Can you take me to the city center?

- Sto cercando un parcheggio. - I am looking for a parking lot.

- È lontano da qui? - Is it far from here?

- Che giorno è oggi? - What day is it today?

- Potrebbe ripetere, per favore? - Could you repeat that, please?

- Quanto è lontano? - How far is it?

- Posso avere una coperta in più? - Can I have an extra blanket?

- Dove posso trovare un negozio di souvenir? - Where can I find a souvenir shop?

- È incluso il servizio di pulizia? - Is cleaning service included?

- Sto cercando una farmacia. - I am looking for a pharmacy.

- È aperto tutto l'anno? - Is it open all year round?

- Vorrei ordinare qualcosa da mangiare. - I would like to order something to eat.

- Come si chiama questo posto in italiano? - What is the name of this place in Italian?

- Dove posso trovare un internet café? - Where can I find an internet café?

- Questo è per me? - Is this for me?

- È vicino qui? - Is it near here?

- Dove posso trovare un bancomat? - Where can I find an ATM?

- Vorrei prenotare un tavolo per due persone. - I would like to book a table for two.

- Quanto tempo ci vuole per arrivare a...? - How long does it take to get to...?

- Posso avere un'altra coperta? - Can I have another blanket?

- Mi può consigliare un buon posto per fare una passeggiata? - Can you recommend a good place for a walk?

- Che ora chiude? - What time does it close?

- Vorrei noleggiare una macchina. - I would like to rent a car.

- Dove posso trovare un negozio di alimentari? - Where can I find a grocery store?

- Vorrei una bottiglia di vino rosso/bianco. - I would like a bottle of red/white wine.

- Mi può aiutare a portare le valigie? - Can you help me with the luggage?

- È possibile fumare qui? - Is it possible to smoke here?

- Posso avere il menu in italiano? - Can I have the menu in Italian?

- È incluso nel prezzo? - Is it included in the price?

- Posso avere un asciugamano in più? - Can I have an extra towel?

- Vorrei una camera con vista sul mare. - I would like a room with a sea view.

- È compreso il parcheggio? - Is parking included?

- Vorrei noleggiare una bicicletta. - I would like to rent a bike.

- Cosa c'è da vedere qui? - What is there to see here?

- È lontano a piedi? - Is it far to walk?

- Che giorno è oggi? - What day is today?

- Quanto costa? - How much does it cost?

- Dove posso trovare un ristorante vegetariano? - Where can I find a vegetarian restaurant?

- Vorrei fare una prenotazione. - I would like to make a reservation.

- Mi potrebbe portare un cuscino in più? - Could you bring me an extra pillow?

- Posso avere una mappa della città? - Can I have a map of the city?

- Quanto è lontano? - How far is it?

- Mi può consigliare un bel posto per fare una passeggiata? - Can you recommend a nice place for a walk?

- Posso avere una coperta in più? - Can I have an extra blanket?

- Dove posso trovare un negozio di souvenir? - Where can I find a souvenir shop?

- È incluso il servizio di pulizia? - Is cleaning service included?

- Sto cercando una farmacia. - I am looking for a pharmacy.
- È aperto tutto l'anno? - Is it open all year round?
- Vorrei ordinare qualcosa da mangiare. - I would like to order something to eat.
- Come si chiama questo posto in italiano? - What is the name of this place in Italian?
- Dove posso trovare un internet café? - Where can I find an internet café?

- Questo è per me? - Is this for me?
- È vicino qui? - Is it near here?
- Dove posso trovare un bancomat? - Where can I find an ATM?
- Vorrei prenotare un tavolo per due persone. - I would like to book a table for two.

- Quanto tempo ci vuole per arrivare a...? - How long does it take to get to...?
- Posso avere un'altra coperta? - Can I have another blanket?
- Mi può consigliare un buon posto per fare una passeggiata? - Can you recommend a good place for a walk?

- Che ora chiude? - What time does it close?
- Vorrei noleggiare una macchina. - I would like to rent a car.
- Dove posso trovare un negozio di alimentari? - Where can I find a grocery store?

- Vorrei una bottiglia di vino rosso/bianco. - I would like a bottle of red/white wine.
- Mi può aiutare a portare le valigie? - Can you help me with the luggage?
- È possibile fumare qui? - Is it possible to smoke here?
- Posso avere il menù in italiano? - Can I have the menu in Italian?
- È incluso nel prezzo? - Is it included in the price?

- Posso avere un asciugamano in più? - Can I have an extra towel?
- Vorrei una camera con vista sul mare. - I would like a room with a sea view.
- È compreso il parcheggio? - Is parking included?
- Vorrei noleggiare una bicicletta. - I would like to rent a bike.

- Cosa c'è da vedere qui? - What is there to see here?
- È lontano a piedi? - Is it far to walk?
- Che giorno è oggi? - What day is today?
- Quanto costa? - How much does it cost?
- Dove posso trovare un ristorante vegetariano? - Where can I find a vegetarian restaurant?

- Mi scusi, potrebbe indicarmi il bagno più vicino? - Excuse me, could you please point me to the nearest restroom?
- Potrebbe chiamare un taxi per me? - Could you call a taxi for me?

- Vorrei ordinare un caffè/macchiato/cappuccino, per favore. - I would like to order a coffee/espresso/cappuccino, please.

- Mi potrebbe dare indicazioni per raggiungere il centro storico? - Could you give me directions to the historic center?
- Ho bisogno di assistenza medica, dove posso trovare un ospedale? - I need medical assistance, where can I find a hospital?
- Vorrei pagare il conto, per favore. - I would like to pay the bill, please.

- Sto cercando un biglietto per un tour guidato. - I am looking for a ticket for a guided tour.
- Mi può consigliare un buon posto per gustare la cucina tradizionale? - Can you recommend a good place to enjoy traditional cuisine?
- Mi scusi, parla inglese? - Excuse me, do you speak English?
- Quanto tempo ci vuole per arrivare alla stazione ferroviaria/aeroporto? - How long does it take to get to the train station/airport?
- Vorrei prenotare un'escursione nella natura. - I would like to book a nature excursion.

- Ho bisogno di cambiare soldi, dove posso trovare un ufficio di cambio? - I need to exchange money, where can I find a currency exchange office?

- Potrebbe suggerirmi un buon posto per fare una passeggiata serale? - Could you suggest a good place for an evening stroll?

- Mi potrebbe aiutare a chiamare un'ambulanza? - Could you help me call an ambulance?

- C'è un servizio di navetta per l'aeroporto? - Is there a shuttle service to the airport?

- Vorrei noleggiare una bicicletta per esplorare la città. - I would like to rent a bike to explore the city.

- Dove posso trovare informazioni turistiche? - Where can I find tourist information?

- Ho perso il mio telefono, potrebbe aiutarmi a rintracciarlo? - I lost my phone, could you help me track it down?

- Potrebbe consigliarmi un bel posto per ammirare il tramonto? - Could you recommend a nice place to watch the sunset?

- Sto cercando un'attività divertente da fare in città. - I am looking for a fun activity to do in the city.

- Vorrei prenotare un tour enogastronomico. - I would like to book a food and wine tour.

- Mi potrebbe consigliare un negozio di souvenir? - Could you recommend a souvenir shop?

- Cosa consiglierebbe di visitare oltre alle attrazioni principali? - What would you recommend to visit besides the main attractions?

- Sto cercando una guida turistica che parli la mia lingua. - I am looking for a tour guide who speaks my language.
- Potrebbe chiamare un'auto per il noleggio? - Could you call a car rental for me?
- Dove posso trovare una farmacia aperta fino a tardi? - Where can I find a pharmacy open late?
- Vorrei saperne di più sulla storia di questa città. - I would like to learn more about the history of this city.

- Ho perso il mio bagaglio, potrebbe aiutarmi a rintracciarlo? - I lost my luggage, could you help me track it down?
- Potrebbe consigliarmi un bel posto per fare una gita fuori porta? - Could you recommend a nice place for a day trip?
- C'è un ufficio turistico qui vicino? - Is there a tourist office nearby?
- Sto cercando un negozio di abbigliamento, potrebbe indicarmene uno? - I am looking for a clothing store, could you point me to one?

- Potrebbe chiamare un taxi per portarmi alla stazione ferroviaria? - Could you call a taxi to take me to the train station?
- Vorrei prenotare un tour in barca lungo la costa. - I would like to book a boat tour along the coast.
- Mi potrebbe consigliare un buon posto per fare una passeggiata in montagna? - Could you recommend a good place for a mountain hike?

- Potrebbe consigliarmi un posto tranquillo dove rilassarsi? - Could you recommend a quiet place to relax?

- Dove posso trovare un centro benessere per una giornata di relax? - Where can I find a spa for a day of relaxation?
- Vorrei noleggiare un'auto per esplorare la regione, potrebbe aiutarmi? - I would like to rent a car to explore the region, could you help me?
- C'è un mercato locale qui vicino? - Is there a local market nearby?

- Potrebbe consigliarmi un buon posto per ascoltare musica dal vivo? - Could you recommend a good place to listen to live music?
- Vorrei prenotare un volo per la prossima destinazione, potrebbe aiutarmi? - I would like to book a flight to the next destination, could you help me?

- Mi potrebbe consigliare un escursione in bicicletta? - Could you recommend a cycling excursion?
- Vorrei noleggiare una barca per una giornata di pesca, è possibile qui? - I would like to rent a boat for a day of fishing, is it possible here?
- Potrebbe chiamare un taxi per portarmi alla stazione degli autobus? - Could you call a taxi to take me to the bus station?

- Vorrei fare un'escursione in montagna, potrebbe consigliarmi un sentiero? - I would like to go hiking in the mountains, could you recommend a trail?
- Potrebbe chiamare un dottore per me? - Could you call a doctor for me?
- Vorrei fare una passeggiata lungo il fiume, dove posso trovare un bel sentiero? - I would like to take a walk along the river, where can I find a nice trail?
- Mi potrebbe consigliare un buon posto per fare un picnic? - Could you recommend a good place for a picnic?

- Sto cercando un buon posto per fare birdwatching, potrebbe aiutarmi? - I am looking for a good place for birdwatching, could you help me?
- Potrebbe consigliarmi un ristorante con cucina vegana/vegetariana? - Could you recommend a restaurant with vegan/vegetarian cuisine?
- Vorrei noleggiare una moto per esplorare la campagna circostante, è possibile qui? - I would like to rent a motorcycle to explore the surrounding countryside, is it possible here?

- C'è un centro sportivo qui vicino? - Is there a sports center nearby?
- Mi potrebbe aiutare a organizzare un tour enologico? - Could you help me organize a wine tour?
- Vorrei fare un'escursione a cavallo, dove posso trovare un maneggio? - I would like to go horseback riding, where can I find a riding stable?

- Potrebbe chiamare un'agenzia di noleggio barche per me? - Could you call a boat rental agency for me?

- Vorrei prenotare un corso di cucina tradizionale, è possibile qui? - I would like to book a traditional cooking class, is it possible here?

- Potrebbe suggerirmi un buon posto per fare snorkeling? - Could you suggest a good place for snorkeling?

- Vorrei noleggiare attrezzatura per fare immersioni subacquee, dove posso trovare un negozio? - I would like to rent scuba diving equipment, where can I find a shop?

- Potrebbe chiamare un servizio di guida turistica per me? - Could you call a tour guide service for me?

- Mi potrebbe consigliare un'esperienza culinaria autentica? - Could you recommend an authentic culinary experience?

- Vorrei prenotare un corso di ceramica, è possibile qui?
- I would like to book a pottery class, is it possible here?

- Potrebbe suggerirmi un bel posto per fare una gita in barca a vela? - Could you suggest a nice place for a sailing trip?

- Vorrei organizzare un picnic romantico, dove posso trovare un bel posto? - I would like to arrange a romantic picnic, where can I find a nice spot?

- Potrebbe chiamare un servizio di trasporto per me? - Could you call a transportation service for me?

- Vorrei noleggiare un kayak per esplorare i laghi della regione, è possibile qui? - I would like to rent a kayak to explore the lakes of the region, is it possible here?

- Potrebbe consigliarmi un bel posto per fare un'escursione fotografica? - Could you recommend a nice place for a photo excursion?

- Vorrei fare un'escursione in mountain bike, dove posso trovare dei sentieri? - I would like to go mountain biking, where can I find some trails?

- Potrebbe aiutarti a prenotare un tour in elicottero? - Could you help me book a helicopter tour?

- Vorrei fare un'escursione in jeep, è possibile qui? - I would like to go on a jeep tour, is it possible here?

- Potrebbe suggerirmi un buon posto per fare parapendio? - Could you suggest a good place for paragliding?

- Vorrei organizzare un viaggio di pesca in mare, potrebbe consigliarmi un'agenzia? - I would like to organize a deep-sea fishing trip, could you recommend an agency?

- Potrebbe chiamare un servizio di noleggio camper per me? - Could you call a camper rental service for me?

- Vorrei fare una passeggiata nel parco naturale, dove posso trovare l'ingresso? - I would like to take a walk in the natural park, where can I find the entrance?

- Potrebbe consigliarmi un buon posto per fare canyoning? - Could you recommend a good place for canyoning?

- Vorrei prenotare un'esperienza di volo in mongolfiera, è possibile qui? - I would like to book a hot air balloon flight experience, is it possible here?

- Potrebbe chiamare un servizio di trasferimento per l'aeroporto per me? - Could you call an airport transfer service for me?

- Vorrei organizzare una gita in famiglia, potrebbe suggerirmi un'attività adatta ai bambini? - I would like to organize a family outing, could you suggest a child-friendly activity?
- Potrebbe consigliarmi un bel posto per fare una passeggiata in barca? - Could you recommend a nice place for a boat ride?
- Vorrei noleggiare una moto d'acqua per una giornata, dove posso trovare un noleggio? - I would like to rent a jet ski for a day, where can I find a rental?
- Potrebbe chiamare un servizio di trasporto per me e il mio cane? - Could you call a transportation service for me and my dog?

- Vorrei fare un'escursione in mongolfiera al tramonto, potrebbe aiutarmi a organizzarla? - I would like to go on a sunset hot air balloon ride, could you help me organize it?
- Potrebbe consigliarmi un bel posto per fare una passeggiata serale romantica? - Could you recommend a nice place for a romantic evening stroll?
- Vorrei prenotare un'esperienza di immersioni notturne, è possibile qui? - I would like to book a night diving experience, is it possible here?
- Potrebbe chiamare un'agenzia di noleggio bici elettriche per me? - Could you call an electric bike rental agency for me?

- Vorrei organizzare un'escursione a cavallo al sorgere del sole, potrebbe aiutarmi? - I would like to organize a sunrise horseback riding excursion, could you help me?

- Potrebbe consigliarmi un bel posto per fare un picnic al chiaro di luna? - Could you recommend a nice place for a moonlit picnic?

- Vorrei prenotare un esperienza di canyoning estremo, è possibile qui? - I would like to book an extreme canyoning experience, is it possible here?

- Potrebbe chiamare un servizio di noleggio attrezzatura subacquea per me? - Could you call a scuba diving equipment rental service for me?

- Vorrei fare un'escursione in kayak al tramonto, dove posso trovare un noleggio? - I would like to go on a sunset kayak excursion, where can I find a rental?

- Potrebbe consigliarmi un bel posto per fare il parapendio all'alba? - Could you suggest a nice place for sunrise paragliding?

- Vorrei organizzare un viaggio di pesca in mare profondo all'alba, potrebbe consigliarmi un'agenzia? - I would like to organize a deep-sea fishing trip at dawn, could you recommend an agency?

- Potrebbe chiamare un servizio di noleggio scooter per me? - Could you call a scooter rental service for me?

- Vorrei fare una passeggiata in bicicletta e degustare vini locali, è possibile qui? - I would like to go on a bicycle ride and taste local wines, is it possible here?

- Potrebbe consigliarmi un bel posto per fare una passeggiata in barca al tramonto? - Could you recommend a nice place for a sunset boat ride?

- Vorrei prenotare un'esperienza di volo in deltaplano, è possibile qui? - I would like to book a hang gliding experience, is it possible here?
- Potrebbe chiamare un servizio di trasporto per me e la mia famiglia? - Could you call a transportation service for me and my family?

- Vorrei organizzare una gita in bicicletta con la mia famiglia, potrebbe aiutarmi? - I would like to organize a family bike ride, could you help me?
- Potrebbe consigliarmi un bel posto per fare trekking? - Could you recommend a nice place for trekking?
- Vorrei prenotare un'esperienza di vela al tramonto, è possibile qui? - I would like to book a sunset sailing experience, is it possible here?

- Potrebbe chiamare un'agenzia di noleggio moto per me? - Could you call a motorcycle rental agency for me?
- Vorrei fare un'escursione in moto alla ricerca di paesaggi mozzafiato, potrebbe consigliarmi un percorso? - I would like to go on a motorcycle excursion in search of breathtaking landscapes, could you recommend a route?
- Potrebbe aiutarti a prenotare un tour fotografico? - Could you help me book a photo tour?

- Vorrei fare un'escursione in jeep attraverso le montagne, è possibile qui? - I would like to go on a jeep tour through the mountains, is it possible here?

- Potrebbe consigliarmi un bel posto per fare parapendio al tramonto? - Could you suggest a nice place for sunset paragliding?
- Vorrei organizzare una gita di pesca notturna in mare, potrebbe consigliarmi un'agenzia? - I would like to organize a night fishing trip at sea, could you recommend an agency?
- Potrebbe chiamare un servizio di noleggio camper per me e i miei amici? - Could you call a camper rental service for me and my friends?
- Vorrei fare un'escursione in kayak al sorgere del sole, dove posso trovare un noleggio? - I would like to go on a sunrise kayak excursion, where can I find a rental?

- Potrebbe consigliarmi un bel posto per fare parapendio alba? - Could you suggest a nice place for sunrise paragliding?
- Vorrei organizzare un viaggio di pesca in mare profondo all'alba, potrebbe consigliarmi un'agenzia? - I would like to organize a deep-sea fishing trip at dawn, could you recommend an agency?
- Potrebbe chiamare un servizio di noleggio scooter per me? - Could you call a scooter rental service for me?
- Vorrei fare una passeggiata in bicicletta e degustare vini locali, è possibile qui? - I would like to go on a
bicycle ride and taste local wines, is it possible here?

- Potrebbe consigliarmi un bel posto per fare una passeggiata in barca al tramonto? - Could you recommend a nice place for a sunset boat ride?

- Vorrei prenotare un'esperienza di volo in deltaplano, è possibile qui? - I would like to book a hang gliding experience, is it possible here?

- Potrebbe chiamare un servizio di trasporto per me e la mia famiglia? - Could you call a transportation service for me and my family?

- Vorrei organizzare una gita in bicicletta con la mia famiglia, potrebbe aiutarmi? - I would like to organize a family bike ride, could you help me?

- Potrebbe consigliarmi un bel posto per fare trekking? - Could you recommend a nice place for trekking?

- Vorrei prenotare un'esperienza di vela al tramonto, è possibile qui? - I would like to book a sunset sailing experience, is it possible here?

- Potrebbe chiamare un'agenzia di noleggio moto per me? - Could you call a motorcycle rental agency for me?

- Vorrei fare un'escursione in moto alla ricerca di paesaggi mozzafiato, potrebbe consigliarmi un percorso?

- I would like to go on a motorcycle excursion in search of breathtaking landscapes, could you recommend a route?

- Potrebbe aiutarti a prenotare un tour fotografico? - Could you help me book a photo tour?

- Vorrei fare un'escursione in jeep attraverso le montagne, è possibile qui? - I would like to go on a jeep tour through the mountains, is it possible here?

- Potrebbe consigliarmi un bel posto per fare parapendio al tramonto? - Could you suggest a nice place for sunset paragliding?

- Vorrei organizzare una gita di pesca notturna in mare, potrebbe consigliarmi un'agenzia? - I would like to organize a night fishing trip at sea, could you recommend an agency?
- Potrebbe chiamare un servizio di noleggio camper per me e i miei amici? - Could you call a camper rental service for me and my friends?
- Vorrei fare un'escursione in kayak al sorgere del sole, dove posso trovare un noleggio? - I would like to go on a sunrise kayak excursion, where can I find a rental?

Slang Terms
- Mavì: A term used to refer to a friend or buddy.
- Specchiarsi: To chill out or relax.
- Ngrasciarsi: To eat a lot or indulge in food excessively.
- Cazzeggio: Hanging out doing nothing in particular.
- Arrangiatu: Resourceful, someone who can always find a solution.
- Cusina: Kitchen, often used to refer to homemade food.

- Ammuina: Let's go, let's move.
- Stato: The police, law enforcement.
- Sfiga: Bad luck or an unfortunate situation.
- Mangiarotti: A big meal, usually a feast.
- Accatari: To buy something, especially impulsively.
- Scoppiato: Crazy or out of control.
- Capo: Boss or leader.

- Figura: Reputation or image.
- Scirocco: Drunk or intoxicated.
- Scassato: Broken or damaged.
- Ammazzare: To kill or destroy, used metaphorically.
- Puffo: A term for someone who is naive or gullible.
- Sbirri: Derogatory term for the police.
- Pischello: A young, inexperienced person.
- Tarantella: A mess or chaotic situation.
- Figo: Cool or awesome.
- Perdere le staffe: To lose one's temper.
- Tirchi: Stingy or cheap.

- Fregare: To cheat or deceive.
- Alcolizzato: Someone who drinks excessively or is an alcoholic.
- Sballo: A wild party or night out.
- Rissa: A fight or brawl.

- Bova: A loud, boisterous person.
- Zompa Cazzate: Talking nonsense or rubbish.
- Tossire: To leave or go away.
- Sparare cazzate: To talk nonsense or bullshit.
- Menare: To hit or beat up.

- Camorra: Trouble or mischief.
- Arrapato: Horny or sexually aroused.
- Scopata: A sexual encounter or hook-up.
- Moccioso: Bratty or spoiled.
- Rompipalle: Annoying or irritating person.

- Rubacuori: Heartthrob or ladies' man.
- Merdoso: Shitty or of poor quality.
- Stronzo: Asshole or jerk.
- Fesso: Fool or idiot.
- Prezzemolo: Someone who is always around or meddling.

- Fesso: Fool or idiot.
- Ceppare: To ignore or brush off someone.
- Andare a farsi benedire: To go to hell or get lost.
- Pucciare: To get drunk.
- Scocciare: To annoy or bother someone.
- Sbronzarsi: To get drunk.

Fat Facts Calabria

Calabria, also known as the "toe" of Italy's boot, is a region rich in history, natural beauty, and cultural charm. It's a land of rocky mountains, pristine beaches, picturesque hilltop towns, and ancient ruins, catering to all types of travellers.

Calabria has a diversified terrain, ranging from the snow-capped heights of the Sila mountains to the turquoise waters of the Ionian and Tyrrhenian Sea. The region is also home to rolling hills, fertile valleys, and stunning canyons, making it an ideal destination for adventure enthusiasts.

Calabria's coastline runs for over 782 km, providing a diverse range of beaches to select from. From Tropea's white sand beaches to Capo Vaticano's rocky coves, there's a great place to swim, sunbathe and participate in water sports.

Mountain Majesty: The Sila mountains, a national park, are ideal for trekking, skiing, and environment enthusiasts. This breathtaking natural paradise offers lush forests, crystal-clear lakes, and beautiful villages to explore.

Hidden Gems: Calabria is dotted with picturesque hilltop towns and villages, each with its own personality and history. Some examples include Gerace, which has a Norman cathedral, and Tropea, which is set on a rock overlooking the sea.

Calabria's Rich History

Calabria's history spans thousands of years, with influences from the Greeks, Romans, Byzantines, and Normans. This complex tapestry is visible in the area's archaeological sites, museums, and traditional architecture.

Ancient Greeks: The Greeks were the first to settle in Calabria, leaving behind remnants such as the Temple of Hera at Locri and the National Archaeological Museum of Reggio Calabria, which holds the famed Riace bronzes.

Roman Legacy: The Romans constructed roads, aqueducts, and amphitheatres throughout Calabria, some of which are still visible today. Scolacium's archaeological site exemplifies this age.

The Normans left their mark on Calabria with castles, fortifications, and cathedrals, including the impressive Castello Aragonese in Reggio Calabria.

A Celebration of flavours: Calabria's culinary delights

Calabrian cuisine is a delectable combination of Mediterranean and indigenous flavours. Fresh fish, veggies, olive oil, and chilli peppers are common ingredients in numerous meals. Some must-try specialties are:

Nduja is a spicy sausage made from pork, chilli peppers and other spices.

Caciocavallo Silano is a DOP-protected cheese manufactured from cow milk in the Sila highlands.
La Morra: A sweet ricotta cake with orange and lemon zest.

To genuinely discover the heart of Calabria, go beyond the big tourist attractions. Here's some suggestions:
Attend a local sagra (festival) to immerse oneself in the local culture, which includes traditional food, music, and dance.
Learn how to make "nduja": Take a cooking lesson and learn how to make this classic Calabrian sausage.
Hike the Sila Mountains: You may explore the stunning scenery of the Sila Mountains on foot or by bicycle.
Go stargazing in Sila National Park. Escape the light pollution and enjoy the breathtaking night sky at Sila National Park.

Calabria provides a wonderful Italian retreat with its breathtaking beauty, rich history, delectable cuisine, and kind friendliness.
So, pack your bags and explore the enchantment of Calabria!

Made in the USA
Las Vegas, NV
10 February 2025